BUMBLEBEE BISTRO
Color Hunting with Daphne Dragonfly

Written by

Anne Brownlow

Dedication

This book is dedicated to the little readers with curious minds and their parents who guide them, to the homesteaders crafting a life of self-sufficiency, and to the novice gardeners planting their first seeds.

May you all find joy and discovery in the pages of this story.

BUMBLEBEE BISTRO
DAPHNE DRAGONFLY

By the pond, where the water's a mirror so clear,
Daphne Dragonfly's colors were about to appear.
She darted and danced, with a flicker and swirl,
Discovering the colors in her own little world.

"Green," in the lily pads, floating with ease,
Where frogs rest and croak, as much as they please.

"Yellow," in the buttercups, kissed by the sun.
Dancing in the breeze, having so much fun.

"Blue," in the sky, vast and so high.
Where the cotton puff clouds sail idly by.

"Pink." in the lotus. blooming with pride.
A home for the fish. that quietly hide.

"Orange," in the goldfish, gliding below.
Their scales catch the light, and put on a show.

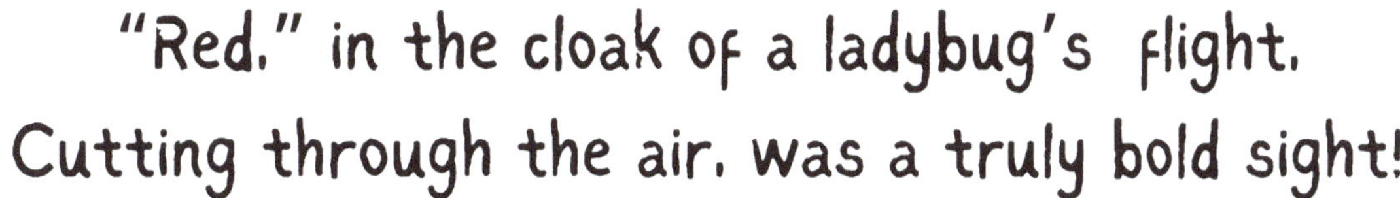

"Red." in the cloak of a ladybug's flight.
Cutting through the air. was a truly bold sight!

"Purple." in the bird. perched by the shore.
It's feathers a sight. impossible to ignore.

"Brown," is the mud, where pond life begins.
A foundation for reeds, among other things.

"Black," in the feathers of a rather loud crow,
Who caws a hello, from up high and down low.

"White," in the swan, so graceful and pure.
Gliding through the water, a sight to ensure.

Daphne Dragonfly's wings hummed with delight.
For the pond's simple colors. shining so bright.
She explored and admired. each hue a rare find.
A tapestry of nature. so wonderfully designed.

As the sun dips low and the day takes its bow.
Daphne Dragonfly feels the evening's soft vow.
The colors fade gently, a whispering light.
A serene transition to the coming night.

Now the stars twinkle on. a silver array,
Daphne rests in the reeds. ending her play.
The moon's gentle glow. a comforting friend.
In the pond's color collection. the day finds its end.

ACTIVITIY PAGES

Don your boots, call your folks, to the meadow we stride.
To the pond where the dragonflies joyfully glide.
For the water's a place where nature's colors are shown,
And together safe with family, its beauty can be known.

POND COLOR COLLECTION

It's time to get creative with the Pond Color Collection! Can you remember all the dazzling shades from Daphne Dragonfly's adventure? Grab your crayons, pencils or paint and bring the picture to life with every color you remember. Let's see how vibrant your adventure can be!

COLOR MATCH QUEST

Can you remember all the colors that Daphne found?
Daphne Dragonfly loves colors, and she has found lots of them! . Now, she needs your help to match them to the correct word.

How to Play:
Trace the dotted line from each color to its matching word. Can you find the right shade for every word? Let's learn and play—match them all today!

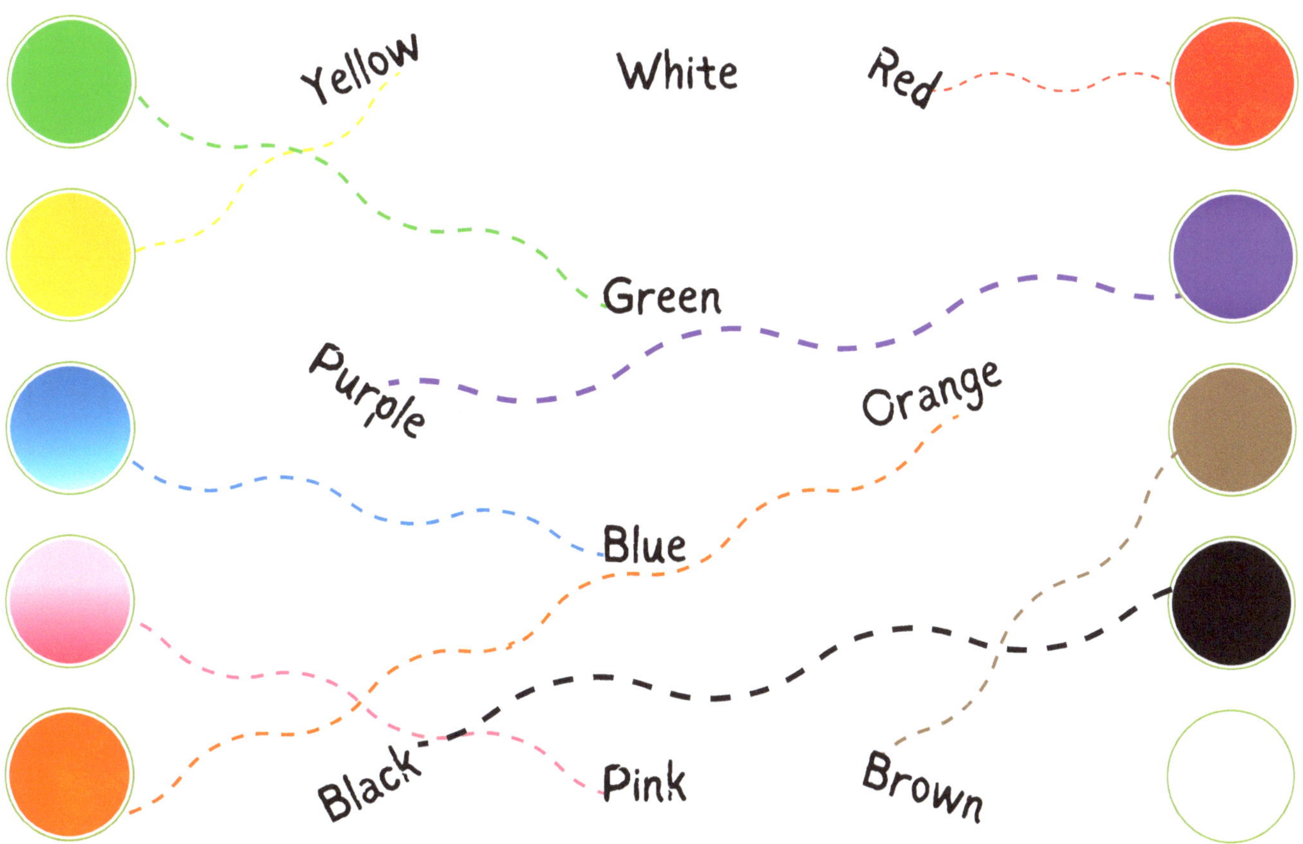

DRAGONFLY DEFENDERS

Did you know that dragonflies only live in places where the water is not polluted, so seeing dragonflies means our ponds and streams are healthy! Here's how you can become a Dragonfly Defender:

Create a Dragonfly Diner: Just like butterflies, dragonflies love to eat. You can help by making sure there are plenty of plants around your pond for them to find food.

Water Wonders: Dragonflies lay their eggs in water, so having a clean pond or stream nearby is perfect for them. You can help by keeping our waters free of trash and pollution.

Be a Dragonfly Defender: Since dragonflies are so important, we need to protect them. You can be a defender by learning more about them and teaching others how cool they are!

Let's make our world a dragonfly delight!

POND PALS

A pond is a place of wonder and discovery! This is where Daphne Dragonfly and her friends have amazing adventures every day. Each creature here has a unique role that helps keep the pond lively and beautiful. Let's dive in and meet these marvelous Pond Pals:

<u>Frogs</u>: These jumpy friends love to croak and hop around lily pads. They help keep insect populations in check and their tadpoles clean the water by eating algae.

<u>Buttercups</u>: Buttercups are like little suns of the meadow. With their bright yellow petals, they light up our landscapes and attract various pollinators, including bees and butterflies. These cheerful flowers are not just pretty to look at; they play a crucial role in ecosystems by supporting biodiversity.

<u>Blue Sky</u>: The sky appears blue because of the way sunlight is scattered by Earth's atmosphere. Blue light waves are shorter and scatter more than other colors, which is why we see a blue sky most of the time

<u>Pink Lotus Blossom</u>: These beautiful flowers are like nature's water filters. They help clean the water in ponds, making it a healthier place for fish and other pond creatures. It is also the national flower of a country called India.

<u>Goldfish</u>: These shimmering swimmers add beauty to our ponds and are a sign of a healthy aquatic ecosystem.

<u>Ladybugs</u>: These tiny beetles with their red cloaks are a gardeners' best friends because they eat aphids and other plant-eating pests.

<u>Purple Birds</u>: Some birds have stunning purple feathers that are very rare in nature. This special color can be seen when the sunlight hits their feathers just right. making them sparkle like little jewels in the trees!

<u>Mud</u>: Mud. glorious mud! As well as being wonderful to splash around in. it's also a superhero for plants and animals! Mud is like a giant sponge that soaks up water and nutrients. It also gives homes to tiny creatures that fish and birds love to eat

<u>Crows</u>: Often misunderstood, crows are very smart and help clean up by eating waste and leftover food.

<u>Swans</u>: Swans remind us of the grace and beauty of nature. They also help control aquatic vegetation, keeping our waterways clear.

<u>Dragonflies</u>: Daphne and her dragonfly friends are important predators of harmful insects and are indicators of a healthy environment.

PONDS

Ponds are like nature's nurseries! They provide a safe place for frogs to lay their eggs, for dragonflies to grow up, and for fish to swim freely. Ponds are full of life, from the tiniest insects skimming the surface to the plants that grow in and around them.

Visiting a pond can be an adventure! You might see ducks paddling, hear frogs croaking, or spot a colorful dragonfly zooming by. And if you look closely, you might even find a hidden world of creatures living in the mud and water.

Taking care of our ponds is important. We can help by keeping them clean and not disturbing the animals that live there.

HEALTHY RECIPES TO MAKE WITH YOUR PARENTS

Mini Crustless Quiches

Ingredients:
Eggs
Milk
Cheese
your choice of veggies
(like spinach, tomatoes, or bell peppers)

Instructions:
Whisk together the eggs and milk.
Stir in chopped veggies and shredded cheese.
Pour into greased muffin tins.
Bake at 180°C (350°F) for 20-25 minutes until set.
Sprinkle on some fresh watercress and enjoy!

This recipe is not only tasty but also fun to eat and are easily packed away in the basket for your picnic adventure!

Ingredients:
Grab an armful of mixed fruit.
Strawberries
Apples
Grapes
Melons
Pineapples

Instructions:
Cut the fruits into bite-sized pieces.
Thread them onto skewers in a colorful pattern.
Keep them chilled until you are ready to go on your picnic.

These are like magic wands filled with yummy fruit! They're bright, sweet, and just right for little hands to hold. Eating them is like going on a tasty rainbow adventure!

These yummy dishes are perfect for a sunny day picnic. The mini quiches are tasty and filling, while the fruit skewers are like a cool breeze of flavors. Together, they make picnic time delicious, fun, and oh-so-refreshing!

THANK YOU!

To all the wonderful children and their amazing grown-ups,

Thank you from the bottom of my heart for joining Daphne Dragonfly on her colorful journey around the pond. It's been a splashing good time discovering all the colors that nature has to offer, hasn't it?

Ponds are enchanting places, brimming with life and a rainbow of colors. They're where dragonflies zoom and dance in the air, and where every ripple in the water tells a story. The next time you're out on an adventure, perhaps you can explore a pond or a stream. Watch the water bugs skate across the surface and look for fish darting below. Keep an eye out for Daphne and her friends as they flit from flower to flower! They're all part of the pond's colorful symphony.

I hope Daphne's story has filled your imagination with vivid colors and has shown you the beauty of our natural world.

With heartfelt thanks and the gentlest of dragonfly wing-hugs,

Anne Brownlow

Until next time.